Famous

Quotations

Revised to be

Gender Neutral

by Naz Marta Zamoyski

First Edition
© 2014   Open Thought Software, Inc

ASIN Number: B00O6WLAK2

Table of Contents

Why the Need for Gender Neutral Language?

Gender equality starts with gender neutral language, because words do matter. All of the famous quotations in this book were originally written using language that was not gender-neutral, also known as "gender-biased", "sexist" or "exclusive" language, written to prefer the masculine gender.

In addition to being simply incorrect, "Professionals in many fields recognize that gender-biased language makes women invisible and constructs an inaccurate world." (See Ref. 1)

This book proudly revises famous quotations that were written using gender-biased language, or making gender role assumptions, to now use gender-neutral language.

In this way, everyone can now feel that each quotation fully applies to them without feeling excluded, and without experiencing a poke in the eye from reading gender biased language.

So I invite everyone to enjoy these timeless words of wisdom, now available for the first time in gender-neutral language. May they bring you much wisdom, inspiration and prosperity!

Dedication

This book is dedicated to all of the people who have fought for gender equality throughout the many centuries of human history.

Special thanks to Emma Watson for carrying the gender equality movement forward at this time in our history, through her role as United Nations Goodwill Ambassador for Gender Equality, and especially for her brilliant and heartfelt speech to the UN in September 2014 where she introduced the #heforshe idea to get everyone involved in fighting for gender equality. (See Ref. 2)

Acknowledgements

To my BFF, Nancy Chavenson, for her unwavering friendship, and for providing the yin to my yang.

To my dear friends and review team: Nancy, Jed, Barbara, Sheila, Dan, Jenn and Eileen.

And to my husband Dan, the love of my life and my soul mate forever, for his love, support and infinite patience.

Timeline of Quotations

Lao Tzu (Born 604 BC)

Buddha (563 BC)

Confucius (551 BC)

Sun Tzu (544 BC)

Socrates (469 BC)

Plato (427 BC)

Aristotle (384 BC)

Chanakya (370 BC)

Horace (65 BC)

Leonardo Da Vinci (1452 AD)

Baruch Spinoza (1632 AD)

John Locke (1632 AD)

Voltaire (1694 AD)

Immanuel Kant (1724 AD)

Napoleon Bonaparte (1769 AD)

Ralph Waldo Emerson (1803 AD)

Abraham Lincoln (1809 AD)

Henry David Thoreau (1817 AD)

Emily Dickinson (1830 AD)

Mark Twain (1835 AD)

Nietzsche (1844 AD)

Oscar Wilde (Born 1854 AD)

Lao Tzu

Also "Laozi" or "Lao-tze"

604 BC to 531 BC

1

One who knows, does not speak.

One who speaks, does not know.

2

Leaders are best

when people barely know they exist,

when the leader's work is done,

the leader's aim fulfilled,

the people will say: we did it ourselves.

3

For the wise look into space

and know there are no limited dimensions.

4

People who control others may be powerful,

but people who have mastered themselves

are mightier still.

5

Whoever is contented is rich.

6

People's enemies are not demons,

but people like themselves.

7

The career of sages is of two kinds:

They are either honored by all in the world,

Like a flower waving its head,

Or else they disappear into the silent forest.

8

Anyone who is too insistent

on their own views,

finds few to agree with them.

9

Whoever talks more is sooner exhausted.

10

Sages do not hoard.

The more sages help others,

the more they benefit themselves,

The more they give to others,

the more they get themselves.

The Way of Heaven does one good

but never does one harm.

The Way of the sage is to act

but not to compete.

11

People in their handling of affairs

often fail when they are about to succeed.

If you remain as careful at the end

as you were at the beginning,

there will be no failure.

12

Whoever obtains has little.

Whoever scatters has much.

13

Whoever conquers others is strong;

Whoever conquers themselves is mighty.

14

How could anyone rejoice in victory

and delight in the slaughter of people?

15

Anyone who does not trust enough,

Will not be trusted.

16

Whoever knows others is wise.

Whoever knows themselves is enlightened.

Buddha

563 BC to 483 BC

1

Whoever loves 50 people has 50 woes;

whoever loves no one has no woes.

2

Just as a candle cannot burn without fire,

people cannot live without a spiritual life.

3

It is a person's own mind,

not their enemy or foe,

that lures them to evil ways.

4

Do not overrate what you have received,

nor envy others.

Whoever envies others

does not obtain peace of mind.

5

To enjoy good health,

to bring true happiness to one's family,

to bring peace to all,

one must first discipline and control

one's own mind.

If a person can control their mind

they can find the way to Enlightenment,

and all wisdom and virtue

will naturally come to them.

6

I do not believe in a fate that falls on people

however they act;

but I do believe in a fate that falls on people

unless they act.

7

What is the appropriate behavior
for any person in the midst of this world,
where each person is clinging
to their piece of debris?
What's the proper salutation between people
as they pass each other in this flood?

Confucius

551 BC to 479 BC

1

If I am walking with two other people,

each of them will serve as my teacher.

I will pick out the good points of the one

and imitate them,

and the bad points of the other

and correct them in myself.

2

The more people meditate

upon good thoughts,

the better will be their world

and the world at large.

3

Whoever learns but does not think, is lost!

Whoever thinks but does not learn

is in great danger.

4

Only the wisest

and stupidest

of people never change.

5

The superior person

understands what is right;

the inferior person

understands what will sell.

6

Wisdom, compassion, and courage

are the three universally recognized

moral qualities of human beings.

7

The expectations of life

depend upon diligence;

mechanics that would perfect their work

must first sharpen their tools.

8

Never give a sword

to a person who can't dance.

9

Superior people are modest in their speech,

but exceed in their actions.

10

Superior people are distressed

by the limitations of their ability;

they are not distressed

by the fact that their ability is not
recognized.

11

Superior people

think always of virtue;

the common people

think of comfort.

12

If you speak without modesty,

you will find it difficult

to make your words good.

13

Whoever exercises government

by means of their virtue

may be compared to the north polar star,

which keeps its place

and all the stars turn towards it.

14

Virtue is not left to stand alone.

Whoever practices it

will have neighbors.

15

I will not be concerned

at other people not knowing me;

I will be concerned

at my own want of ability.

16

Superior people

make the difficulty to be

overcome their first interest;

success only comes later.

17

Look at the means which people employ,

consider their motives,

observe their pleasures.

People simply cannot conceal themselves!

Sun Tzu

544 BC to 496 BC

1

Whoever knows when they can fight

and when they cannot,

will be victorious.

2

All people can see these tactics

whereby I conquer,

but what none can see

is the strategy

out of which victory is evolved.

3

Whoever is prudent

and lies in wait for an enemy who is not,

will be victorious.

4

Pretend inferiority

and encourage other's arrogance.

5

The opportunity to secure ourselves

against defeat

lies in our own hands,

but the opportunity of defeating the enemy

is provided by the enemy themselves.

6

Generals who win the battle

make many calculations in their temple

before the battle is fought.

The general who loses

makes but few calculations beforehand.

7

Generals who advance

without coveting fame

and retreat without fearing disgrace,

whose only thought

is to protect their country

and do good service for their sovereign,

are the jewels of the kingdom.

8

If you are far from the enemy,

make them believe you are near.

9

Thus it is that in war

the victorious strategist only seeks battle

after the victory has been won,

whereas one who is destined to defeat

first fights and afterwards looks for victory.

10

Now the reason the enlightened prince

and the wise general

conquer the enemy whenever they move

and their achievements surpass

those of ordinary people

is foreknowledge.

11

Hence that general is skillful in attack

whose opponent does not know

what to defend;

and that general is skillful in defense

whose opponent does not know

what to attack.

12

If we know that our own people

are in a condition to attack,

but are unaware that the enemy

is not open to attack,

we have gone only halfway towards victory.

Socrates

469 BC to 399 BC

1

You are richest

if you are content with the least,

for content is the wealth of nature.

2

I am the wisest person alive,

for I know one thing,

and that is that I know nothing.

3

Let whoever that would move the world

first move themselves.

4

It is people of courage

who do not run away,

but remain at their post

and fight against the enemy.

5

Employ your time in improving yourself

by other people's writings,

so that you shall gain easily

what others have labored hard for.

6

An honest person is always a child.

7

All people's souls are immortal,

but the souls of the righteous

are immortal and divine.

8

The end of life

is to be like God,

and the soul following God

will be like God.

9

I was really too honest

to be a politician and live.

10

One who is injured

ought not to return the injury,

for on no account

can it be right to do an injustice;

and it is not right to return an injury,

or to do evil to any person,

however much we have suffered from them.

11

If people are proud of their wealth,

they should not be praised

until it is known how they employ it.

12

As to marriage or celibacy,

let people take which course they will,

they will be sure to repent.

Plato

427 BC to 347 BC

1

Wise people speak

because they have something to say;

Fools because they have to say something.

2

We can easily forgive a child

who is afraid of the dark;

the real tragedy of life

is when people are afraid of the light.

3

A hero is born among a hundred,

a wise person is found among a thousand,

but an accomplished person

might not be found

even among a hundred thousand people.

4

Someone who was wise invented beer.

5

The direction in which education

starts a person

will determine their future in life.

6

The measure of anyone

is what they do with power.

7

For a person to conquer themselves

is the first and noblest of all victories.

8

Someone who commits injustice
is ever made more wretched
than someone who suffers it.

9

The blame is theirs who choose:
God is blameless.

10

People who make everything
that leads to happiness
depend upon themselves,
and not upon others,
have adopted the very best plan
for living happily.
These are the people of moderation,
the people of character and of wisdom.

11

All people are by nature equal,

made all of the same earth by one Worker;

and however we deceive ourselves,

as dear unto God is the poor peasant

as the mighty prince.

12

There are three classes of people;

lovers of wisdom,

lovers of honor,

and lovers of gain.

13

Whoever is not a good servant

will not be a good master.

14

Justice means minding your own business

and not meddling with other people's
concerns.

15

The punishment which the wise suffer

who refuse to take part in the government,

is to live under the government

of worse people.

16

When there is an income tax,

the just person will pay more

and the unjust less

on the same amount of income.

17

Whoever is of calm and happy nature

will hardly feel the pressure of age,

but to those of an opposite disposition

youth and age are equally a burden.

18

Rhetoric

is the art of ruling the minds of people.

19

Nothing in the affairs of human beings

is worthy of great anxiety.

20

No one should bring children into the world
who is unwilling to persevere to the end
in their nature and education.

21

When people speak ill of you,
live so as nobody may believe them.

22

Humans: Beings in search of meaning.

23

People who steal a little
steal with the same wish
as people who steal much,
but with less power.

24

Death is not the worst
that can happen to people.

25

No evil can happen to a good person,
either in life or after death.

26

Any person may easily do harm,

but not every person can do good to another.

27

Human beings are wingless animals

with two feet and flat nails.

28

People never legislate,

but destinies and accidents,

happening in all sorts of ways,

legislate in all sorts of ways.

29

This and no other

is the root from which tyrants spring;

when they first appear

they are protectors.

30

It is right to give every person their due.

31

All things will be produced

in superior quantity and quality,

and with greater ease,

when each person works at a single occupation,

in accordance with their natural gifts,

and at the right moment,

without meddling with anything else.

32

One person

cannot practice many arts with success.

33

Truth is the beginning

of every good to the gods,

and of every good to humans.

34

Then not only an old person,

but also a drunkard,

becomes a second time a child.

35

The gods' service is tolerable,

human's intolerable.

36

States are as the people,

they grow out of human characters.

37

Whatever deceives people

seems to produce a magical enchantment.

38

There's a victory, and defeat;

the first and best of victories,

the lowest and worst of defeats

which each person gains or sustains

at the hands not of another,

but of themselves.

Aristotle

384 BC to 322 BC

1

My best friend is the person

who in wishing me well

wishes it for my sake.

2

At best,

humans are the noblest of all animals;

separated from law and justice

they are the worst.

3

Hope is the dream of a waking person.

4

Democracy is when the indigent,

and not the property owners,

are the rulers.

5

The ideal person

bears the accidents of life

with dignity and grace,

making the best of circumstances.

6

I count someone braver

who overcomes their desires

than someone who conquers their enemies;

for the hardest victory is over self.

7

To run away from trouble

is a form of cowardice and,

while it is true that suicides brave death,

they do it not for some noble object

but to escape some ill.

8

Jealousy

is both reasonable

and belongs to reasonable people,

while envy is base and belongs to the base,

for the one

makes you get good things by jealousy,

while the other

does not allow your neighbor to have them

through envy.

9

Wise people

do not expose themselves needlessly

to danger,

since there are few things

for which they care sufficiently;

but they are willing, in great crises,

to give even their life -

knowing that under certain conditions

it is not worthwhile to live.

10

Whoever is unable to live in society,

or who has no need

because they are self-sufficient,

must be either a beast or a god

11

A tyrant must put on the appearance

of uncommon devotion to religion.

Subjects are less apprehensive

of illegal treatment

from a ruler whom they consider

god-fearing and pious.

On the other hand,

subjects do less easily move

against such rulers,

believing that these rulers

have the gods on their side.

12

All people by nature desire knowledge.

13

In general,

people are naturally apt to be swayed

by fear rather than reverence,

and to refrain from evil

rather because of the punishment

that it brings

than because of its own foulness.

14

Humans are by nature political animals.

15

It is unbecoming for youth to utter maxims.

16

No one loves the people they fear.

17

People acquire a particular quality

by constantly acting in a particular way.

18

Whoever has many friends has none.

19

For one swallow does not make a summer,

nor does one day;

and so too one day, or a short time,

does not make a person blessed and happy.

20

Whoever is to be a good ruler

must have first been ruled.

21

Perfect friendship

is the friendship of people who are good,

and alike in excellence;

for these wish well alike

to each other qua good,

and they are good in themselves.

22

Different people seek after happiness

in different ways and by different means,

and so make for themselves

different modes of life

and forms of government.

23

People are swayed more by fear

than by reverence.

24

It is clearly better that property

should be private,

but the use of it common;

and the special business of the legislator

is to create in people

this benevolent disposition.

25

Without friends

no one would choose to live,

though they had all other goods.

Chanakya

Traditionally identified as:
Kautilya or Vishnu Gupta

370 BC to 283 BC

1

People are great by their deeds,

not by their birth.

2

There is poison in the fang of the serpent,

in the mouth of the fly

and in the sting of a scorpion;

but wicked people are saturated with it.

3

Those who live in our mind are near

though they may actually be far away;

but those who are not in our heart are far

though they may really be nearby.

4

The life of an uneducated person
is as useless as the tail of a dog
which neither covers its rear end,
nor protects it from the bites of insects.

5

People who are overly attached
to their family members
experience fear and sorrow,
for the root of all grief is attachment.
Thus one should discard attachment
to be happy.

6

We should not fret for what is past,
nor should we be anxious about the future;
People of discernment
deal only with the present moment.

7

As a single withered tree, if set aflame,

causes a whole forest to burn,

so does a rascal child

destroy a whole family.

8

The wise should restrain their senses

like the crane

and accomplish their purpose

with due knowledge

of their place, time and ability.

9

The one excellent thing

that can be learned from a lion

is that whatever you intend to do

should be done by you

with a whole-hearted and strenuous effort.

Horace

Full Name:
Quintus Horatius Flaccus

65 BC to 8 BC

1

Lawyers are people

who hire out their words and anger.

2

Pale Death beats equally

at the gates of the poor

and at the palaces of kings.

3

Undeservedly you will atone for the sins

of your family ancestors.

4

It is of no consequence

of what parents you were born,

as long as you are a person of merit.

5

If your fortune does not fit you,

it is like the shoe in the story;

if too large it trips you up,

if too small it pinches you.

6

We rarely find anyone who can say

they have lived a happy life,

and who, content with their life,

can retire from the world

like a satisfied guest.

7

If you postpone the hour of living

then you are like the rustics

who wait for the river to run out

before they cross.

8

Who then is free?

Wise people who can command themselves.

9

A portion of humanity

take pride in their vices

and pursue their purpose;

many more waver

between doing what is right

and complying with what is wrong.

10

You will gain everyone's approval

if you mix the pleasant

with the useful.

11

You have not lived badly

if your birth and death

have been unnoticed by the world.

Leonardo da Vinci

Full Name:
Leonardo di ser Piero da Vinci

1452 AD to 1519 AD

1

The greatest deception people suffer

is from their own opinions.

2

If you love practice without theory

you are like sailors

who board ships

without a rudder and compass

and never know where they may cast.

3

Whoever wishes to be rich in a day

will be hanged in a year.

4

People who conduct an argument

by appealing to authority

are not using their intelligence;

they are just using their memory.

5

Lofty geniuses

when they are doing the least work

are most active.

6

I have offended God and humanity

because my work

didn't reach the quality it should have.

Baruch Spinoza

1632 AD to 1677 AD

1

Desire is the very essence of a person.

2

Pride is pleasure

arising from a person's thinking

too highly of themselves.

3

They alone are free

who live with free consent

under the entire guidance of reason.

4

How would it be possible

if salvation were ready to our hand,

and could without great labor be found,

that it should be

by almost all people neglected?

But all things excellent

are as difficult as they are rare.

5

People govern nothing with more difficulty

than their tongues,

and can moderate their desires

more than their words.

6

Fame has also this great drawback,

that if we pursue it,

we must direct our lives

so as to please the fancy of others.

John Locke

1632 AD to 1704 AD

1

All humanity...

being all equal and independent,

no one ought to harm another

in their life, health, liberty or possessions.

2

The reason why people enter into society

is the preservation of their property.

3

There cannot be greater rudeness

than to interrupt another

in the current of their discourse.

4

It is of great use to sailors
to know the length of their lines,
though they cannot with it fathom
all the depths of the ocean.

5

Education begins the gentleman and lady,
but reading, good company and reflection
must finish them.

6

No one's knowledge here
can go beyond their experience.

7

Everyone has a property
in their own person.
Nobody has a right to this,
but themselves.

8

I have always thought the actions of people
the best interpreters of their thoughts.

9

All people are liable to error;

and most people are, in many points, by
passion or interest,

under temptation to it.

10

It is one thing to show someone

that they are in an error,

and another

to put them in possession of the truth.

11

An excellent person, like precious metal,

is in every way invariable;

A villain, like the beams of a balance,

is always varying, upwards and downwards.

12

To prejudge other people's notions

before we have looked into them

is not to show their darkness

but to put out our own eyes.

13

A sound mind in a sound body,

is a short, but full description

of a happy state in this World:

those that have these two,

have little more to wish for;

and those that want either of them,

will be little the better for anything else.

14

Any one reflecting upon

the thought they have of the delight,

which any present or absent thing

is apt to produce in them,

has the idea we call love.

15

Our deeds disguise us.

People need endless time

to try on their deeds,

until each knows the proper deeds

for them to do.

But every day, every hour, rushes by.

There is no time.

16

I attribute the little I know

to my not having been ashamed

to ask for information,

and to my rule of conversing

with all descriptions of people

on those topics that form

their own peculiar professions and pursuits.

17

There is frequently more to be learned

from the unexpected questions of a child

than the discourses of adults.

Voltaire

Full Name:
François-Marie Arouet

1694 AD to 1778 AD

1

You are free at the moment you wish to be.

2

Every person is guilty
of all the good they did not do.

3

We must cultivate our own garden.
When we were put in the garden of Eden
we were put there so that we should work,
which proves that we were not born to rest.

4

It is better to risk saving a guilty person
than to condemn an innocent one.

5

Superstition is to religion
what astrology is to astronomy:
the mad child of a wise parent.
These children have too long
dominated the earth.

6

It is lamentable,
that to be a good patriot
one must become the enemy
of the rest of humanity.

7

To believe in God is impossible
Not to believe in God is absurd.

8

Use, do not abuse...
neither abstinence nor excess
ever renders us happy.

9

People hate the individual

whom they call avaricious

only because

nothing can be gained from that individual.

10

I have lived eighty years of life

and know nothing for it,

but to be resigned and tell myself

that flies are born to be eaten by spiders

and humans to be devoured by sorrow.

11

People use thought

only as authority for their injustice,

and employ speech

only to conceal their thoughts.

12

All of us are born

with a nose and five fingers,

but no one is born

with a knowledge of God.

13

The first step, my child,

which you make in the world,

is the one on which

depends the rest of your days.

14

There are truths which are not for all people,

nor for all times.

15

Satire lies about literary people

while they live

and eulogy lies about them

when they die.

16

In every author

let us distinguish

the person from the work.

17

If you do not have the spirit of this age,

you have all the misery of it.

Immanuel Kant

1724 AD to 1804 AD

1

In law people are guilty

when they violate the rights of others.

In ethics they are guilty

if they only think of doing so.

2

Whoever is cruel to animals

becomes hard also

in their dealings with people.

We can judge the heart of a person

by their treatment of animals.

3

By a lie,

a human...

annihilates their dignity

as a human being.

4

If someone makes themselves a worm

they must not complain

when they are trodden on.

5

Even philosophers will praise war

as ennobling humanity,

forgetting the Greek who said:

'War is bad in that it begets more evil

than it kills.'

6

From such crooked wood

as that which people are made of,

nothing straight can be fashioned.

Napoleon

Bonaparte

1769 AD to 1821 AD

1

You must not fight too often with one enemy,

or you will teach them all your art of war.

2

The battlefield is a scene of constant chaos.

The winners will be the ones

who control that chaos,

both their own and the enemy's.

3

Never interrupt your enemy

when they are making a mistake.

4

People will fight harder

for their interests

than for their rights.

5

There are only two forces that unite people -

fear and interest.

6

Someone strong is able to intercept at will

the communication

between the senses and the mind.

7

When small people attempt great
enterprises,

they always end by reducing them

to the level of their mediocrity.

8

People are more easily governed

through their vices

than through their virtues.

9

Whoever fears being conquered

is sure of defeat.

10

We must laugh at humanity

to avoid crying for humanity.

11

To do all that one is able to do,

is to be a human being;

to do all that one would like to do,

is to be a god.

12

There is one kind of robber

whom the law does not strike at,

and who steals

what is most precious to us: Time.

13

A true human being hates no one.

Ralph Waldo

Emerson

1803 AD to 1882 AD

1

Shallow people believe in luck.

Strong people believe in cause and effect.

2

The age of a person doesn't mean a thing.

The best tunes are played

on the oldest fiddles.

3

In the morning

we walk with our whole body;

in the evening, only with our legs.

4

People love to wonder,

and that is the seed of science.

5

Adopt the pace of nature:

nature's secret is patience.

6

Heroes are no braver than ordinary people,

but they are brave five minutes longer.

7

People are what their parents made them.

8

Great people are they who see that spiritual

is stronger than any material force -

that thoughts rule the world.

9

Every book is a quotation;

and every house is a quotation

out of all forests,

and mines, and stone quarries;

and every person is a quotation

from all their ancestors.

10

When nature has work to be done,

nature creates a genius to do it.

11

Every genius inspires us

with a boundless confidence

in our own powers.

12

The revelation of thought

takes us out of servitude into freedom.

13

It is one of the beautiful compensations

in this life

that no one can sincerely try to help another

without helping themselves.

14

A great person is always willing to be little.

15

People are what their parents made them.

16

Every actual State is corrupt.

Good people must not obey laws too well.

17

We are born believing.

A person bears beliefs

as a tree bears apples.

18

Happy is the hearing one;

unhappy the speaking one.

19

There is a blessed necessity

by which the interest of humanity

is always driving them to the right;

and, again, making all crime mean and ugly.

20

Trust people

and they will be true to you;

treat them greatly

and they will show themselves great.

Abraham Lincoln

1809 AD to 1865 AD

1

Whenever I hear anyone arguing for slavery,

I feel a strong impulse

to see it tried on them personally.

2

No one has a good enough memory

to be a successful liar.

3

Nearly all people can stand adversity,

but if you want to test a person's character,

give them power.

4

I am not bound to win,

but I am bound to be true.

I am not bound to succeed,

but I am bound to live

by the light that I have.

I must stand with anybody that stands right,

and stand with someone while they are right,

and part with them when they go wrong.

5

We the people are the rightful masters

of both Congress and the courts,

not to overthrow the Constitution

but to overthrow the people

who pervert the Constitution.

6

Let not those who are houseless

pull down the house of another,

but let them work diligently

and build one for themselves,

thus by example assuring that their own

shall be safe from violence when built.

7

No one is good enough

to govern another

without the other's consent.

8

The things I want to know are in books;

my best friend is the one

who'll get me a book I ain't read.

9

These people ask for just the same thing,

fairness, and fairness only.

This, so far as in my power,

they, and all others, shall have.

10

If there is anything
that a person can do well,
I say let them do it.
Give them a chance.

11

The best way to destroy an enemy
is to make them a friend.

12

You have a right to criticize,
if you have a heart to help.

13

Allow presidents
to invade neighboring nations,
whenever they shall deem it necessary
to repel an invasion,
and you allow them
to do so whenever they may choose
to say they deem it necessary
for such a purpose -
and you allow them to make war at pleasure.

14

Discourage litigation.

Persuade your neighbors to compromise

whenever you can.

As a peacemaker

the lawyer has superior opportunity

of being a good person.

There will still be business enough.

15

Whoever molds the public sentiment...

makes statutes and decisions

possible or impossible to make.

16

Every one is said to have

their peculiar ambition.

Whether it be true or not,

I can say for one

that I have no other so great

as that of being truly esteemed

of my kindred human beings,

by rendering myself worthy of their esteem.

17

I like to see a person

proud of the place in which they live.

I like to see a person live

so that their place will be proud of them.

18

The shepherd drives the wolf from the sheep

for which the sheep thank the shepherd

as their liberator,

while the wolf denounces them

for the same act

as the destroyer of liberty.

Plainly, the sheep and the wolf

are not agreed upon a definition of liberty.

19

The way for a young person to rise

is to improve themselves

in every way they can,

never suspecting that anybody

wishes to hinder them.

20

Our defense is in the preservation

of the spirit

which prizes liberty as a heritage

of all people,

in all lands, everywhere.

Destroy this spirit

and you have planted the seeds of despotism

around your own doors.

21

When I am getting ready

to reason with someone,

I spend one-third of my time

thinking about myself

and what I am going to say

and two-thirds about them

and what they are going to say.

22

You have to do your own growing

no matter how tall your grandparents were.

23

I don't like that person.

I must get to know them better.

24

When I hear a person preach,

I like to see them act

as if they were fighting bees.

25

I do not think much of a person

who is not wiser today than yesterday.

26

Books serve to show a person

that those original thoughts of theirs

aren't very new at all.

27

I care not much for a person's religion

whose dog and cat are not the better for it.

28

The time comes upon every public person

when it is best for them

to keep their lips closed.

29

Surely God would not have created

such a being as a human,

with an ability to grasp the infinite,

to exist only for a day!

No, no, humans were made for immortality.

30

Never stir up litigation.

A worse person can scarcely be found

than one who does this.

31

When you have got an elephant

by the hind legs

and they are trying to run away,

it's best to let them run.

32

I don't know who my grandparents were;

I am much more concerned to know

what their grandchild will be.

Charles Darwin

1809 AD to 1882 AD

1

A person who dares to waste

one hour of time

has not discovered the value of life.

2

People's friendships

are one of the best measures of their worth.

3

An American monkey,

after getting drunk on brandy,

would never touch it again,

and thus is much wiser than most people.

4

We must, however, acknowledge,

as it seems to me,

that people with all their noble qualities...

still bear in their bodily frame

the indelible stamp of their lowly origin.

5

It is a cursed evil to any person

to become as absorbed in any subject

as I am in mine.

6

Humanity tends to increase

at a greater rate

than their means of subsistence.

7

Moral beings are ones who are capable

of reflecting on their past actions

and their motives -

of approving of some

and disapproving of others.

Henry David

Thoreau

1817 AD to 1862 AD

1

The most I can do for my friend
is simply be their friend.

2

If one advances confidently
in the direction of their dreams,
and endeavors to live the life
which they have imagined,
they will meet with a success
unexpected in common hours.

3

People have become the tools of their tools.

4

Many people go fishing all of their lives

without knowing

that it is not fish they are after.

5

Every creature is better alive than dead,

humans and moose and pine trees,

and those who understand it aright

will rather preserve its life than destroy it.

6

Do not hire someone

who does your work for money,

but someone who does it for love of it.

7

If someone does not keep pace

with their companions,

perhaps it is because

they hear a different drummer.

Let them step to the music which they hear,

however measured or far away.

8

I have never found a companion

that was so companionable as solitude.

We are for the most part more lonely

when we go abroad among others

than when we stay in our chambers.

A person thinking or working

is always alone,

let them be where they will.

9

The mass of people lead lives

of quiet desperation.

What is called resignation

is confirmed desperation.

10

It is what a person thinks of themselves

that really determines their fate.

11

A person cannot be said

to succeed in this life

who does not satisfy one friend.

12

The person who goes alone can start today;
but whoever travels with another
must wait till that other is ready.

13

I know of no more encouraging fact
than the unquestionable ability of humans
to elevate their lives
by conscious endeavor.

14

Why should we be in such desperate haste
to succeed,
and in such desperate enterprises?
If a person does not keep pace
with their companions,
perhaps it is because they hear
a different drummer.

15

I am sorry to think that you do not get

a person's most effective criticism

until you provoke them.

Severe truth

is expressed with some bitterness.

16

People have a respect

for scholarship and learning

greatly out of proportion

to the use they commonly serve.

17

Most of the luxuries

and many of the so-called comforts of life

are not only not indispensable,

but positive hindrances

to the elevation of humanity.

18

The young person

gets together their materials

to build a bridge to the moon,

or, perchance,

a palace or temple on the earth,

and, at length, the middle-aged person

concludes to build a woodshed with them.

19

A person is rich

in proportion to the number of things

they can afford to let alone.

20

All this worldly wisdom

was once the unamiable heresy

of some wise people.

21

If I knew for a certainty

that someone was coming to my house

with the conscious design of doing me good,

I should run for my life.

22

In the long run,

people hit only what they aim at.

Therefore, they had better aim

at something high.

23

That person is rich

whose pleasures are the cheapest.

24

There is no more fatal blunderer

than someone who consumes

the greater part of their life getting their living.

25

The savage in humans

is never quite eradicated.

26

The Artist is one

who detects and applies the law

from observation of the works of Genius,

whether of Humans or Nature.

The Artisan is one

who merely applies the rules

which others have detected.

27

A person's interest in a single bluebird

is worth more

than a complete but dry list

of the fauna and flora of a town.

28

It is an interesting question

how far

people would retain their relative rank

if they were divested

of their clothes.

29

Some are reputed sick and some are not.

It often happens that the sicker

is the nurse to the sounder.

30

How can any one be weak

who dares to be at all?

31

If a person constantly aspires

are they not elevated?

32

People are born to succeed,

not to fail.

Emily Dickinson

1830 AD to 1886 AD

1

Behavior is what people do,

not what they think, feel, or believe.

2

Because I could not stop for death,

Death kindly stopped for me;

The carriage held but just ourselves

and immortality.

3

They ate and drank the precious Words,

their Spirits grew robust;

They knew no more that they were poor,

nor that their frames were Dust.

4

They say that God is everywhere,

and yet we always think of God

as somewhat of a recluse.

5

I do not like the one

who squanders life for fame;

give me the one

who living makes a name.

Friedrich Nietzsche

1844 AD to 1900 AD

1

Whoever fights monsters

should see to it that in the process

they do not become a monster.

2

The surest way to corrupt youth

is to instruct them to hold in higher esteem

those who think alike

than those who think differently.

3

The person of knowledge must be able

not only to love their enemies

but also to hate their friends.

4

Whoever has a why to live

can bear almost any how.

5

Whoever would learn to fly one day

must first learn to stand and walk and run

and climb and dance;

one cannot fly into flying.

6

Hope in reality is the worst of all evils

because it prolongs our torments.

7

Are humans one of God's blunders?

Or is God one of human's blunders?

8

When one has not had a good parent,

one must create or procure one.

9

Go up close to your friends,

but do not go over to them!

We should also respect

the enemy in our friends.

10

The most common lie

is that which one lies to themselves;

lying to others is relatively an exception.

11

After coming into contact

with someone religious

I always feel I must wash my hands.

12

In every real adult

a child is hidden that wants to play.

13

Good writers possess

not only their own spirit

but also the spirit of their friends.

14

When a hundred people stand together,

each of them loses their mind

and gets another one.

15

Anyone who has declared someone else

to be an idiot, a bad apple,

is annoyed when it turns out in the end

that they weren't.

16

Great indebtedness

does not make people grateful, but vengeful;

and if a little charity is not forgotten,

it turns into a gnawing worm.

17

No one lies so boldly

as the person who is indignant.

18

Genteel people suppose

that those things do not really exist

about which it is impossible

to talk in polite company.

19

Many people fail as original thinkers

simply because their memory is too good.

20

Fanatics are picturesque,

humanity would rather see gestures

than listen to reasons.

21

Of all that is written,

I love only what a person has written

with their own blood.

22

Not when truth is dirty,

but when it is shallow,

do enlightened people

dislike to wade into its waters.

23

Every person

is a creative cause of what happens,

a primum mobile

with an original movement.

24

Once spirit was God,

then it became human,

and now it is even becoming mob.

25

Whoever cannot give anything away

cannot feel anything either.

26

In the consciousness of the truth

you have perceived,

you now see everywhere

only the awfulness

or the absurdity of existence

and loathing seizes you.

27

Whoever laughs best today,

will also laugh last.

28

Every church is a stone

on the grave of a god-person:

it does not want them to rise up again

under any circumstances.

29

Regarding life,

the wisest people of all ages

have judged alike:

it is worthless.

30

Whoever despises themselves

nonetheless respects themselves

as one who despises.

31

Whoever has witnessed another's ideal

becomes their inexorable judge

and as it were their evil conscience.

32

Whoever that humbles themselves
wishes to be exalted.

33

Whoever feels predestined to see
and not to believe
will find all believers too noisy and pushy,
and guards against them.

34

Whoever has provoked people
to rage against them
has always gained a party in their favor, too.

35

What then in the last resort
are the truths of humanity?
They are the irrefutable errors of humanity.

36

What is good?
All that heightens the feeling of power,
the will to power,
power itself in human beings.

37

In the course of history,

we come to see

that iron necessity

is neither iron nor necessary.

Mark Twain

Real Name:
Samuel Langhorne Clemens

1835 AD to 1910 AD

1

The fear of death

follows from the fear of life.

A person who lives fully

is prepared to die at any time.

2

A person's character

may be learned

from the adjectives

which they habitually use in conversation.

3

When people do not respect us

we are sharply offended;

yet in our private heart

we do not much respect ourselves.

4

Humor is humanity's greatest blessing.

5

Clothes make the person.

Naked people

have little or no influence on society.

6

The person who does not read good books

has no advantage

over the person who cannot read them.

7

What a wee little part of a person's life

are their acts and their words!

Their real life is led in their head,

and is known to none but themselves.

8

Humans were made

at the end of the week's work

when God was tired.

9

A person is never more truthful

than when they acknowledge

themselves a liar.

10

If humans could be crossed with cats,

it would improve humans

but deteriorate cats.

11

It is just like human's vanity

and impertinence

to call an animal dumb

because the animal is dumb

to human dull perceptions.

12

A person cannot be comfortable

without their own approval.

13

Humans are the only animals that blush -

or need to.

14

The person who is a pessimist before 48

knows too much;

if the person is an optimist after it,

they know too little.

15

Round people cannot be expected to fit

in a square hole right away.

They must have time to modify their shape.

16

They are now rising

from affluence to poverty.

17

Ideally a book would have no order to it,

and the reader

would have to discover their own.

18

People will do many things
to get themselves loved,
they will do all things
to get themselves envied.

Oscar Wilde

Full Name:
Oscar Fingal O'Flahertie Wills Wilde

1854 AD to 1900 AD

1

Gentlemen and ladies

never hurt anyone's feelings unintentionally.

2

The typewriting machine,

when played with expression,

is no more annoying than the piano

when played by a child or near relation.

3

If you can dominate a London dinner-table

you can dominate the world.

4

Dreamers are those

who can only find their way by moonlight,

and their punishment is

that they see the dawn

before the rest of the world.

5

People are least themselves

when they talk as themselves.

Give them a mask,

and they will tell you the truth.

6

I choose my friends for their good looks,

my acquaintances for their good characters,

and my enemies for their intellects.

You cannot be too careful

in the choice of your enemies.

7

No great artists ever see things

as they really are.

If they did, they would cease to be artists.

8

Some people's faces

are their autobiography.

Other people's faces

are their work of fiction.

9

What is a cynic?

Someone who knows the price of everything

and the value of nothing.

10

We are made to be loved,

not understood.

THE END

of

Volume 1

References

1. University of San Francisco Law Review, "Framing Gender: Federal Appellate Judges' Choices About Gender-Neutral Language", Judith D. Fischer, Winter 2009, Gender-Neutral Language, Article on pages 473 through 506, inclusive. (Words in quote marks appear on pages 475 and 504.)

    Link to article cited in Reference 1:

    http://usf.usfca.edu/law/academic/journals/lawreview/printissues/v43i3/Fischer.pdf

2. Link to speech given by Emma Watson to the United Nations in September 2014:

    https://www.youtube.com/watch?v=p-iFl4qhBsE#t=35

Claimer and Disclaimer

All of the sayings in this book are based on famous quotations made throughout history by a wide variety of authors, and credit is not claimed for these original sayings by this book.

The original work that this book claims is to rewrite each famous quotation to now use gender-neutral language, in a way that reads smoothly and naturally, without drawing attention to the revision.

The utmost regard is given to retain as much of the original language as possible, and to keep the original meaning and sentiment of the famous quotation intact, in a scholarly attempt to preserve great works, while raising them to today's expectation of gender-neutral language. This also includes the ability to "keep the beat" when rewriting poetry or musical lyrics to be gender-neutral.

About the Author

Naz was born and raised on the family farm in Lawrenceville, New Jersey to Polish immigrants who fled from war-torn Europe to the USA before the communist takeover of Poland. Naz was educated at Boston University, where she volunteered at the BU Women's Center and became active in fighting for LGBT, minority and women's rights.

Influenced by social activist Professor Howard Zinn while at BU, Naz switched her major to Political Science, and actively fought for the issues of the day by demonstrating at Boston City Hall, the State House and the Federal Building for the Equal Rights Amendment for women (ERA), and to reverse the unjust guilty verdict of Dr. Kenneth Edelin.

After graduating with a B.S.B.A., Naz was the first woman hired as a software engineer in the US office of a global company in Wellesley, MA. Later, Naz earned her M.S. in Telecommunications from Southern Methodist University, School of Engineering and Applied Science, Department of Electrical Engineering, and has worked as a Computer Engineer professionally for 35 years, where she continued to advocate for LGBT, minority and women's rights in a male-dominated workplace.

She has a patent pending, as sole inventor, from her work as a Distinguished Member of Technical Staff at Alcatel-Lucent (Bell Labs) in Murray Hill, NJ, where she worked on Wireless 2G, 3G, and 4G LTE R&D, and is currently pursuing fresh opportunities with Open Thought Software, Inc.

www.ingramcontent.com/pod-product-compliance
Lightning Source LLC
Chambersburg PA
CBHW050356290526
45786CB00003B/1009